Assembly Instructions

Mounting on Cardboard

This book contains material for two completely separate dioramas, Jurassic and Cretaceous. To make each diorama durable, mount the following pieces on lightweight cardboard (such as oaktag): front panel, background, outer right side, outer left side, floor. For the pages containing the front panel and the outer side panels, be sure to cut away the pieces that are not to be glued onto cardboard (individual dinosaurs and plants; inner side panels).

For mounting, use a white glue such as Elmer's Glue-All. It dries very quickly, so you must work rapidly. Spread the glue over the cardboard (not over the paper). You can achieve an even coating by pouring the glue onto the surface and spreading the glue evenly with a squeegee made of a 2″ × 4″ piece of cardboard. Place the unprinted side of each piece to be glued on the cardboard and press down, using a clean 2″ × 4″ cardboard squeegee to remove any air pockets or wrinkles. Take care to prevent the glue from spreading onto the printed side; keep a wet sponge or damp rag handy to wipe away excess glue if necessary. Once you have spread the piece onto the cardboard and checked to see that there is no glue on the printed side, position a sheet of waxed paper over the piece, then place a weight, such as a heavy book, on top of it. Set aside for at least 15 minutes or until the glue has dried.

To cut out the individual pieces, use an X-Acto knife or matt knife and a steel-edged ruler. If you have never used an X-Acto knife, be careful; the blade is extremely sharp! Practice using the knife on scrap cardboard first. To protect your table or desk, prepare a disposable work

DIORAMA ASSEMBLY DIAGRAM

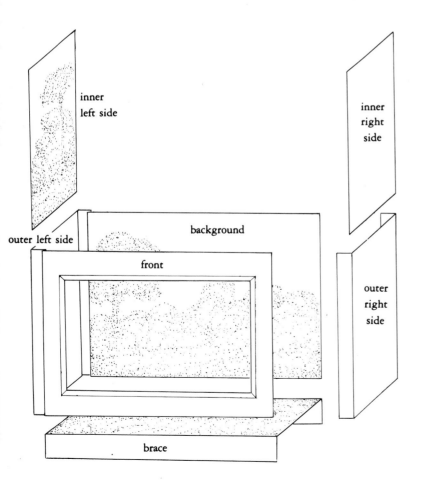

surface on which to cut out the pieces, since you will be cutting completely through the cardboard mounting. Use a large sheet of plywood or heavy cardboard; hold it in position with a pair of lightweight C-clamps or wood clips to prevent slippage while cutting. The outer side pieces can be carefully cut along the solid black lines using a pair of large scissors.

Hints

Read through all the instructions carefully before beginning the assembly, then follow the instructions in the exact order given. Before gluing any of the parts together, check for proper positioning and fit. Follow the exploded Diorama Assembly Diagram for proper orientation of the pieces. The colored sides of the front panel and of the outer side panels face outward.

Scoring

Gently score the dotted fold lines on the floor and the outer side panels by lightly tracing the lines with an X-Acto knife held against a metal-edged ruler. Score lines should not cut through the piece more than halfway. Bend the pieces gently along the score lines so the floor stands on its braces and so the blank sides of the outer side panels are on the inside of the "U" thus formed.

Assembly

With blank surfaces facing one another, glue the inner left side to the outer left side between the scored foldlines; keep the top and bottom edges flush. Repeat for the right side. Let dry.

Glue the front (left-hand) flap of the outer left side to the *wrong* side of the front panel, making a 90° angle at the corner. Glue the back (right-hand) flap of the outer left side *behind* the background as shown in the assembly diagram. Glue the front (right-hand) flap of the outer right side to the wrong side of the front panel, and the back (left-hand) flap behind the background. Spread glue over the braces of the floor, position the diorama over the floor and gently lower it into position, making sure that all bottom edges are flush; glue front brace to back of front panel, and back brace to front of background. Let dry thoroughly.

Dinosaur and Plant Cutouts

Using a pair of curved cuticle scissors or very fine straight scissors, cut around the dinosaur and plant shapes. For complicated areas that may be too fragile if cut closely, leave the shaded background areas in place. After the entire piece has been cut, including the tabs, bend the tabs along the dotted fold lines. Follow the Tab Assembly Diagram to overlap the tabs; this will enable the cutouts to stand securely. Glue or tape the overlapped tabs together for added security.

TAB ASSEMBLY DIAGRAM

For some of the larger dinosaurs, the tabs will not be long enough to overlap one another at the back; these cutouts will stand simply by bending the tabs along the fold lines as for the smaller cutouts. If desired, cut a ¼″-wide strip of waste paper from this book and tape or glue to the tabs of the larger cutouts. Overlap and secure as described above.

Description of Periods and Dinosaurs

The Mesozoic Era began about 200 million years ago and ended about 70 million years ago; it encompassed three periods: Triassic (early), Jurassic (middle) and Cretaceous (late). The first dinosaurs evolved during the Triassic period; dinosaurs reached their peak during the Jurassic period. During the early part of the Cretaceous period, dinosaurs multiplied and diversified, only to become extinct by the end of the period. With this book, you will be able to recreate scenes from the Jurassic and Cretaceous periods, complete with the dinosaurs and vegetation that existed during those times.

Dinosaurs were reptiles; the name means "terrible lizard." Since dinosaurs are known only through their fossilized remains, definite characteristics are difficult to prove. However, much can be discovered by studying where the fossils were found and what was around them, by scrutinizing preserved footprints and other tracks, and by examining fossilized vegetation that existed at the same time.

Because of the wealth of fossilized bones that have been found, scientists have been able to divide dinosaurs into two groups based on

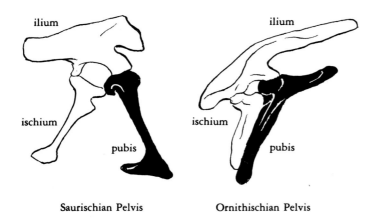

Saurischian Pelvis   Ornithischian Pelvis

differences in their pelvic bones. The saurischian (sawr-ISS-kee-an, "lizard pelvis") group contains dinosaurs with pelvic bones arranged like those of a reptile. The ornithischian (or-nith-ISS-kee-an, "bird pelvis") group consists of dinosaurs with pelvic bones that resemble those of a bird (see diagram). The saurischian dinosaurs were meat and plant eaters; the ornithischian dinosaurs ate only vegetation. The following chart shows the subdivisions of the dinosaur groups that are covered in this book.

Saurischians
Theropods (THEER-o-pods, "beast feet")
Sauropodamorphs (sawr-o-PODE-a-morfs, "lizard-foot forms")

Ornithischians
Ornithopods (OR-nith-o-pods, "bird feet")
Ankylosaurs (AN-kil-o-sawrs, "crooked or curved lizards")
Stegosaurs (STEG-o-sawrs, "plated lizards")
Ceratopsians (ser-a-TOP-see-ans, "horn faces")

Plates 1–3

The Jurassic Period occurred about 160 million years ago and lasted for about 30 million years. The climate during this period was warm and wet, enabling ferns, horsetails and cycads to flourish. Dinosaurs reached their zenith at this time when well-known creatures such as the Stegosaurus (Plate 1, lower left) and the Brontosaurus (Plate 1, in water

and right) freely roamed the earth. (See Plate 6 for a description of the Brontosaurus, and Plate 7 for the Stegosaurus.) The first small mammals appeared, as did feathered, reptilian birds and flying reptiles such as the Rhamphorhynchus (Plate 1, upper left).

Rhamphorhynchus (ram-fo-RINK-us, "prow beak") was an early type of pterosaur (TER-o-sawr, "winged lizard"). The head was large in relation to the rest of the body, with enormous eye sockets and jaws that held many teeth. Wings of skin stretching from the abdomen to the tip of a long fourth finger enabled Rhamphorhynchus to glide on air currents. A flat disc attached to the end of a long tail may have served as a steering device.

Plate 4

Ceratosaurus (cer-at-o-SAWR-us, "horned lizard") was a powerful and savage hunter with a blade-like horn on its nose and bony knobs above the eyes. Clawed fore and hind feet and massive jaws with many long, sharp teeth made this theropod a formidable predator.

Hypsilophodon (hip-si-LOFF-o-don, "high-crested tooth") was herbivorous, feeding primarily on fruit and leaves. Light in weight, Hypsilophodon was bipedal and is thought to have been a very fast runner; this running ability may account for the fact that this ornithopod survived much longer than many of its larger relatives. Its name alludes to the position of a small row of upper teeth.

Scelidosaurus (sel-id-o-SAWR-us, "limb lizard") was a lumbering plant eater with a small head and weak jaws. Covered with bony plates from the head down to the tip of the tail, as well as down the center of the back, Scelidosaurus may have been the ancestor of the Stegosaurus or the Ankylosaurus or both; more fossils must be found before a definitive answer can be determined, although this dinosaur is presently classified as an ankylosaur.

Matonidium (mat-o-NID-ee-um) plants were quite common during the Jurassic period.

Plate 6

Ornitholestes (or-nith-o-LES-tes, "bird robber") was a fast-moving, bipedal carnivore that fed on birds, small mammals and lizards. About six feet in height, Ornitholestes was light in weight with a small skull and long tail. Relatively long arms with clawed fingers enabled this theropod to grasp its prey.

Archaeopteryx (ar-kee-OP-ter-ix, "ancient wing") is the oldest fossil bird on record. Though it had many reptilian features such as teeth, a long bony tail and a wing with clawed fingers, Archaeopteryx was a primitive bird because of the presence of feathers and a wishbone. Weak flight muscles indicate that the bird could not fly, although it was capable of gliding. Several excellent fossils have enabled paleontologists to reconstruct this bird in accurate and complete detail.

Brontosaurus (bront-o-SAWR-us, "thunder lizard") is probably the best-known dinosaur. Also called Apatosaurus (a-pat-o-SAWR-us, "deceptive lizard") this sauropodamorph was about 70 to 80 feet in length and weighed about 20 tons. An enormous body tapered into a long neck and a thick, strong tail. A very small head with the nostrils on top and weak spoon-shaped teeth indicate that Brontosaurus fed on soft aquatic plants. Traces of Brontosaurus footprints show that these huge dinosaurs moved in herds.

Camptosaurus (CAMP-to-sawr-us, "flexible lizard") was a duckbill dinosaur that subsisted on vegetation. It is believed that this heavy, bulky ornithopod walked on all four legs, rearing up on its strong hind legs to feed or run from danger. A long, heavy tail balanced the dinosaur while it was standing.

During the Jurassic period, ferns, cycads (SIGH-kads) and horsetails were quite common.

text continues on the inside back cover

Jurassic Period: Background

Plate 1

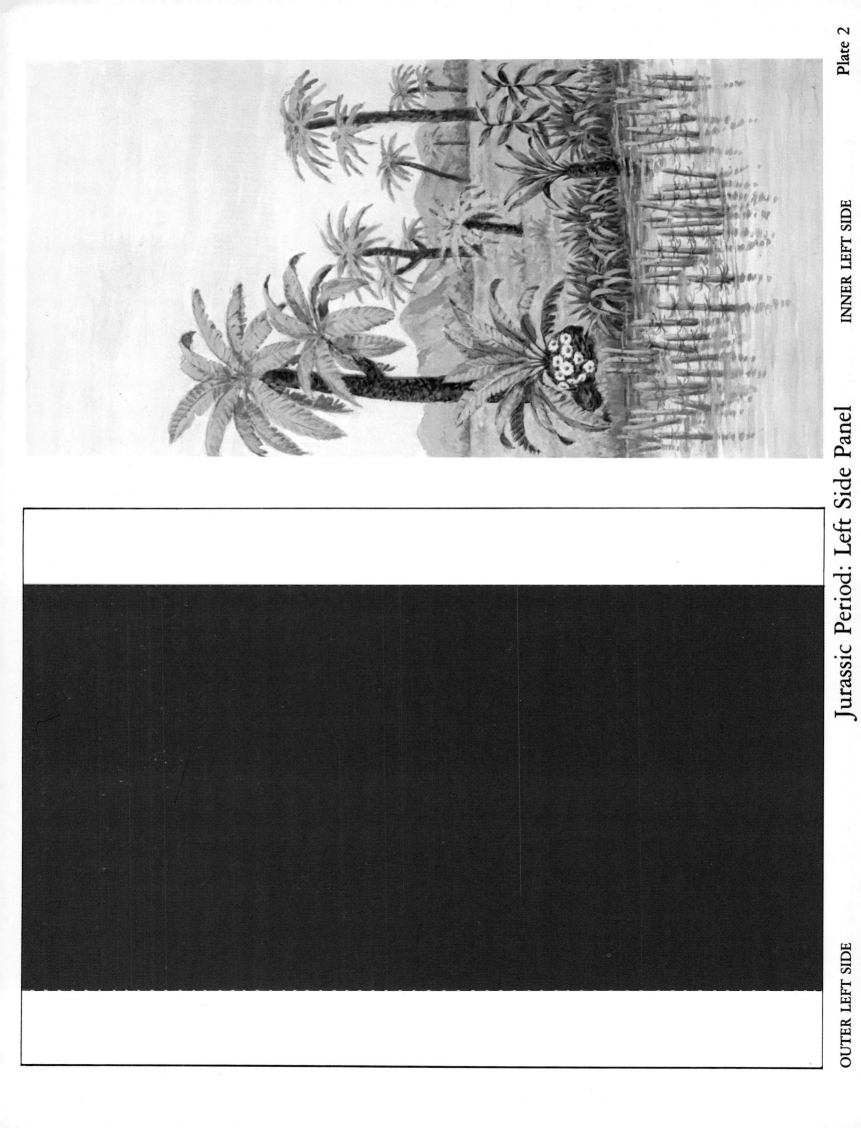

Plate 2

Jurassic Period: Left Side Panel

INNER LEFT SIDE

OUTER LEFT SIDE

Jurassic Period: Right Side Panel   OUTER RIGHT SIDE   Plate 3

INNER RIGHT SIDE

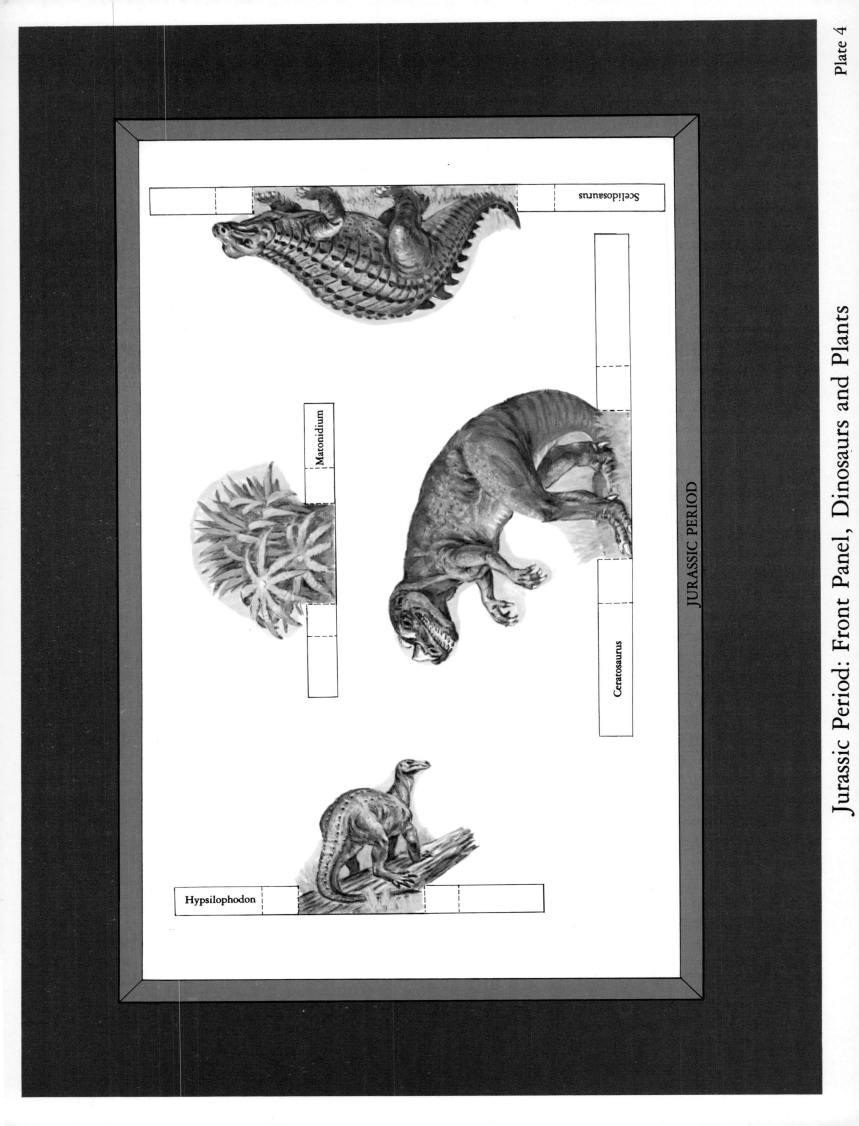

Jurassic Period: Front Panel, Dinosaurs and Plants

Plate 4

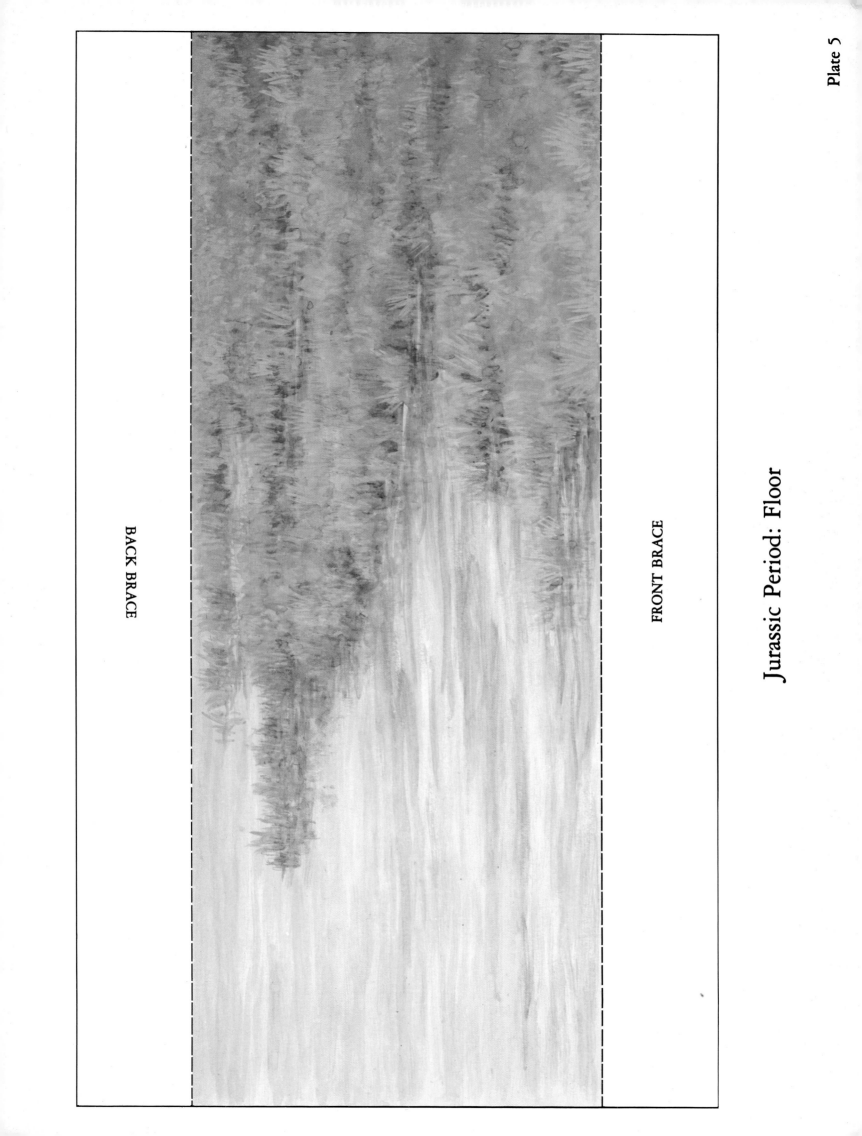

BACK BRACE

FRONT BRACE

Jurassic Period: Floor

Plate 5

Plate 6

Archaeopteryx

Cycad

Camptosaurus

Ferns

Horsetails

Brontosaurus

Archaeopteryx

Ornitholestes

Jurassic Period: Dinosaurs and Plants

Williamsonia

Allosaurus

Cycad

Stegosaurus

Camarasaurus

Plate 7

Jurassic Period: Dinosaurs and Plants

Cretaceous Period: Background

Plate 8

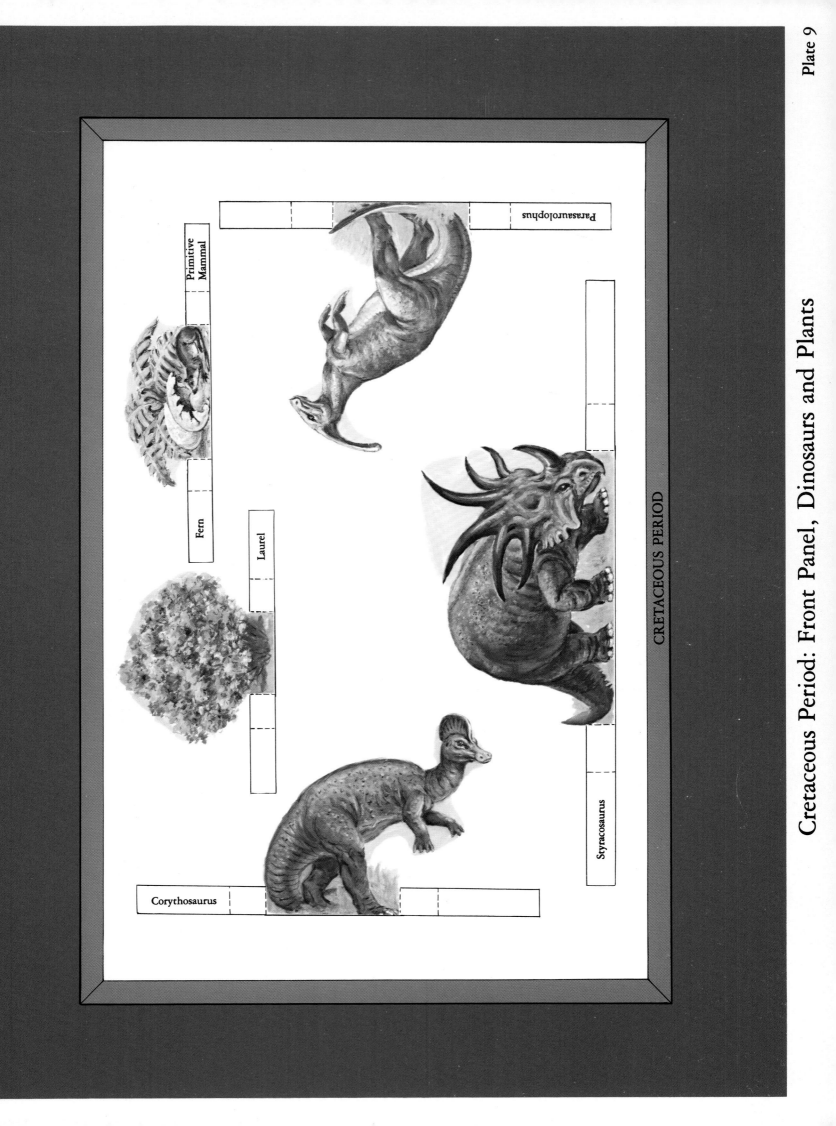

Cretaceous Period: Front Panel, Dinosaurs and Plants

Plate 9

Plate 10

INNER LEFT SIDE

Cretaceous Period: Left Side Panel

OUTER LEFT SIDE

Cretaceous Period: Right Side Panel

Plate 11

OUTER RIGHT SIDE

INNER RIGHT SIDE

Tree

Fern

Laurel

Iguanodon

Ankylosaurus

Trachodon

Cretaceous Period: Dinosaurs and Plants

Plate 12

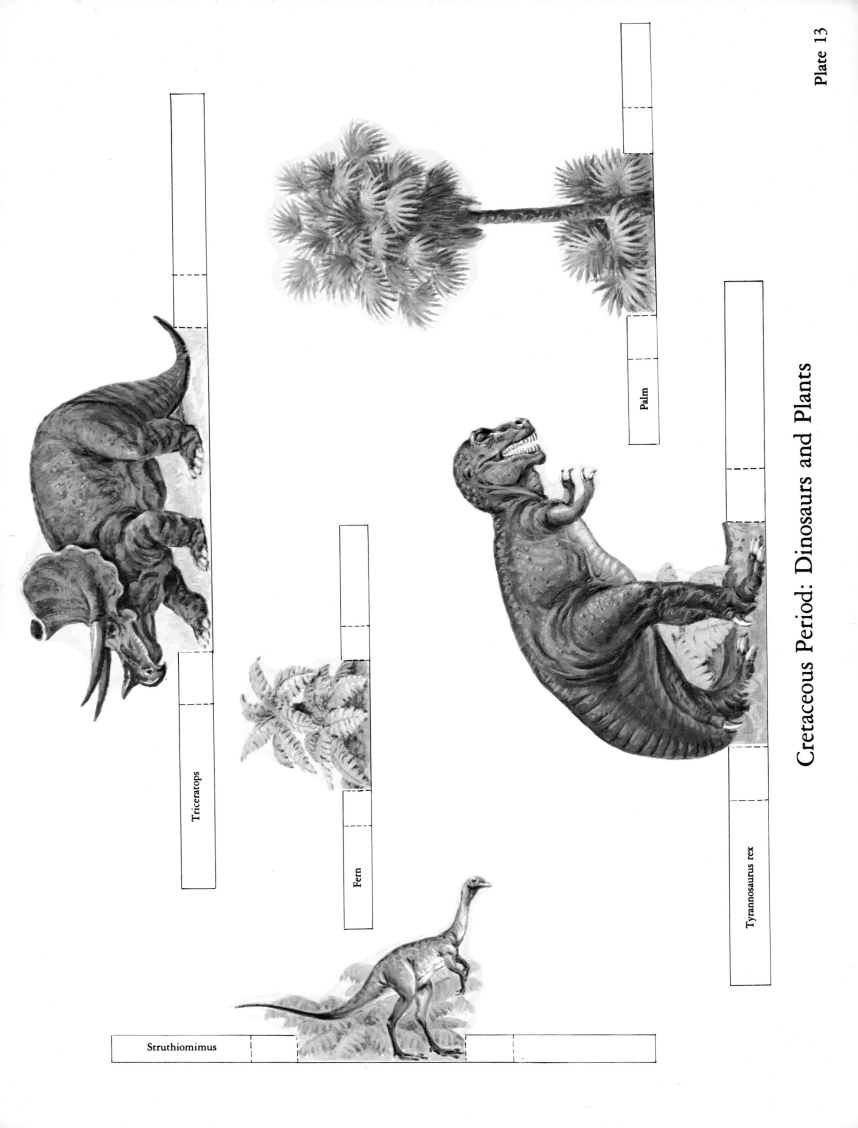

Triceratops

Palm

Fern

Tyrannosaurus rex

Struthiomimus

Cretaceous Period: Dinosaurs and Plants

Plate 13